EDDIE WOO'S
WONDERFUL
WORLD OF
STEM

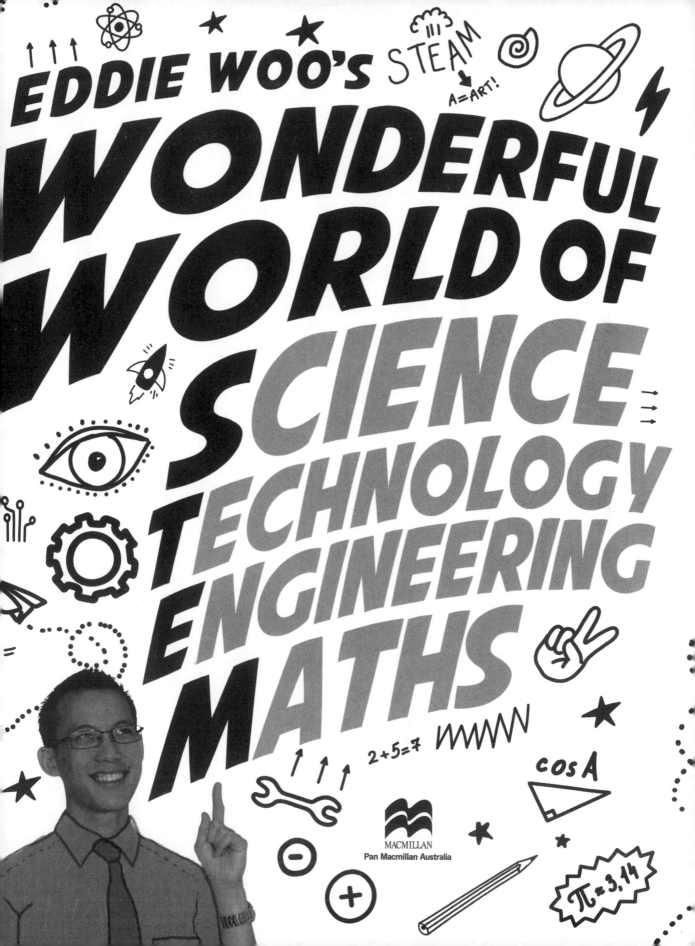

Pan Macmillan acknowledges the Traditional Custodians of Country throughout Australia and their connections to lands, waters and communities. We pay our respect to Elders past and present and extend that respect to all Aboriginal and Torres Strait Islander peoples today. We honour more than sixty thousand years of storytelling, art and culture.

First published 2023 in Macmillan by Pan Macmillan Australia Pty Ltd
1 Market Street, Sydney, New South Wales, Australia, 2000

 A catalogue record for this book is available from the National Library of Australia

Cover and text design by Alissa Dinallo
Cover illustrations courtesy of Shutterstock
Internal illustrations by Alissa Dinallo

Images on pages 1,2, 10, 11, 26, 27, 46, 47, 48, 49, 59, 61, 68, 88, 91, 103, 130, 123, 133, 134, 137, 139, 140 and 156 courtesy of Shutterstock.

Printed in China by Hang Tai Printing Co. Ltd.

To Judy Anderson. Thank you for teaching me
how to be a teacher – and for being such an inspirational
leader in STEM education over the years.

CONTENTS

Eddie Woo teaches mathematics at Cherrybrook Technology High School, Sydney. He has been teaching mathematics for more than fifteen years.

In 2012, Eddie started recording his lessons and uploading them to YouTube – creating 'Wootube'. Since then, he has amassed a following of more than 1.7 million subscribers and his videos have been viewed more than 150 million times.

In 2018, Eddie was named Australia's Local Hero of the Year and shortlisted as one of the top ten teachers in the world.

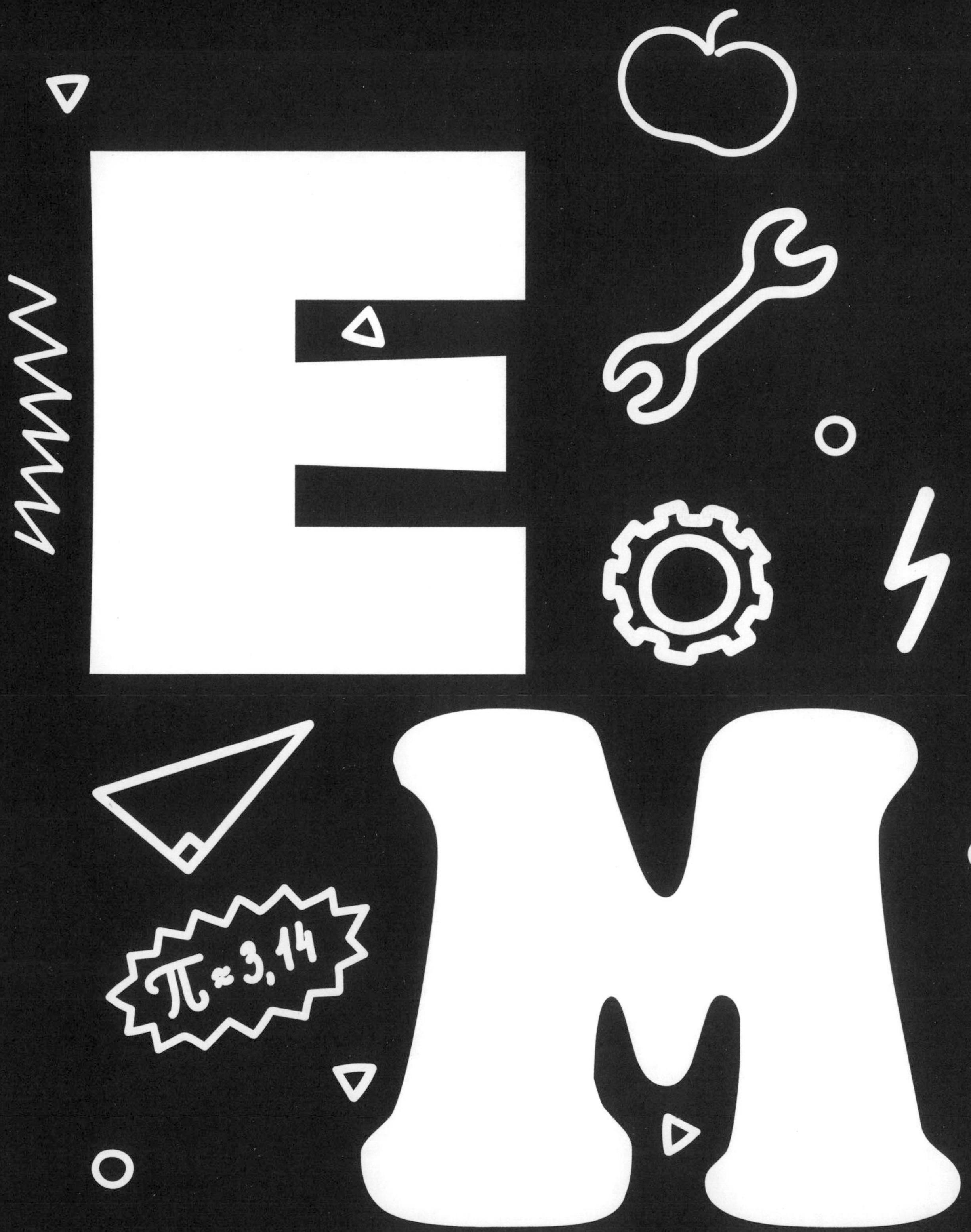
E
M
π ≈ 3,14

I've also set up an easy reference tab system, so you know INSTANTLY which part of the STEM umbrella you're under for each chapter.

A NOTE TO THE READER

This book was made for you to have **FUN** and learn amazing things about the wonders and magic of STEM.

Feel free to scribble and make notes all over the pages.

There are plenty of fun activities to do. Look out for the activity symbols throughout:

You'll find all the answers to these activities in a TOP SECRET section at the back of the book.
DO NOT PEEK.

Most importantly, don't forget that
STEM IS FUN!

STEM

is an acronym.

It stands for . . .

SCIENCE TECHNOLOGY ENGINEERING MATHS

These subjects sound **separate** but they're not.
They weave into and around each other.

We need maths to understand science, such as physics and chemistry.
We need science to understand engineering,
such as how to build bridges.

EVERYTHING IS CONNECTED

In fact . . .

STEM fits a whole lot of other subjects beneath it:

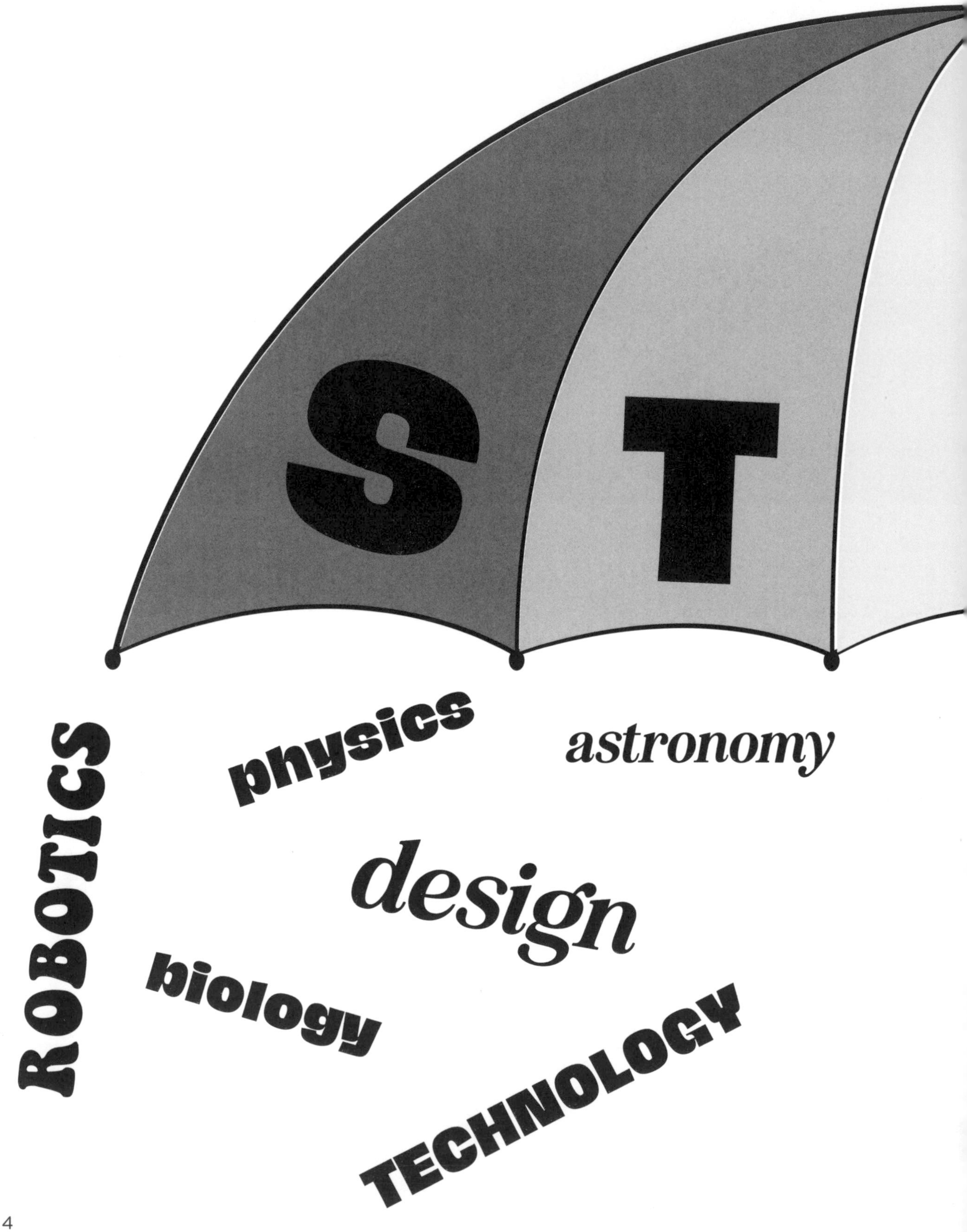

S T

ROBOTICS

physics

astronomy

design

biology

TECHNOLOGY

E M

MATHS

meteorology

coding

geography

GEOLOGY

ACRONYM ALERT

A What do all these acronyms mean?

RADAR _____

SCUBA _____

DNA _____

BASIC _____

LASER _____

LED _____

ET _____

ROYGBIV _____

NASA _____

ASAP _____

BRB _____

PDF _____

FOMO _____

RAM _____

Find all the acronyms in this word search

Q B A R A D F N S X B U P O Z R
W A T G S G E T Z Q F O M O C O
R S P H A H B A Q D Q Q S L S Y
E I S W P J V O S H E D N A Z G
P C R A D A R P D Q U N G H I B
G P A D O K C I F D Q L D K A I
D L O L I L X L G S K J B O R V
A Z C J U Z Z U E A L G R I M P
P L P D F U S Z O D L I B Y L W
R A M T B S O L J Z A A F R U E
P I O Q W G A T K X S R I W T Y
L A S E R X S R L C A Q S A X V
N F I P U Q C E P V N S D V R B
E K A O L D U S O M A T M D P Q
B S H R W N B P I T S Y B S G S
A E L X Q M A E U Y A I C N H K

ON THE MOVE

Technology

Engineering

Maths

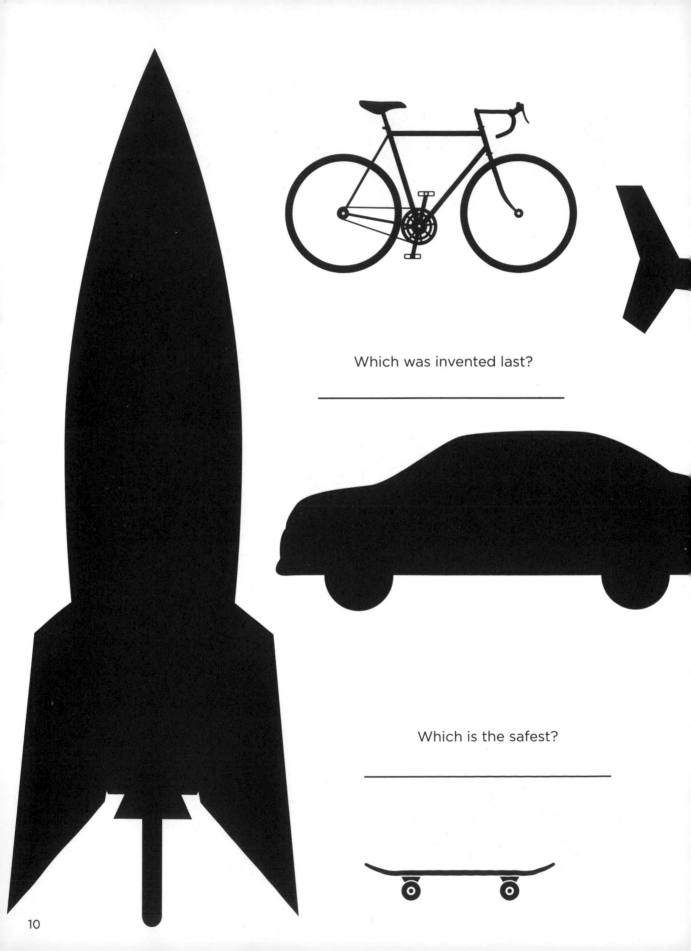

Which was invented last?

_____

Which is the safest?

_____

People use vehicles to get around quickly and easily, and to carry heavy loads. Some vehicles are powered by the people who use them, while others use engines to go further and faster. Life would be much slower without all these vehicles.

Which was invented first?

_____

Which travels furthest?

Which travels fastest?

_____

_____

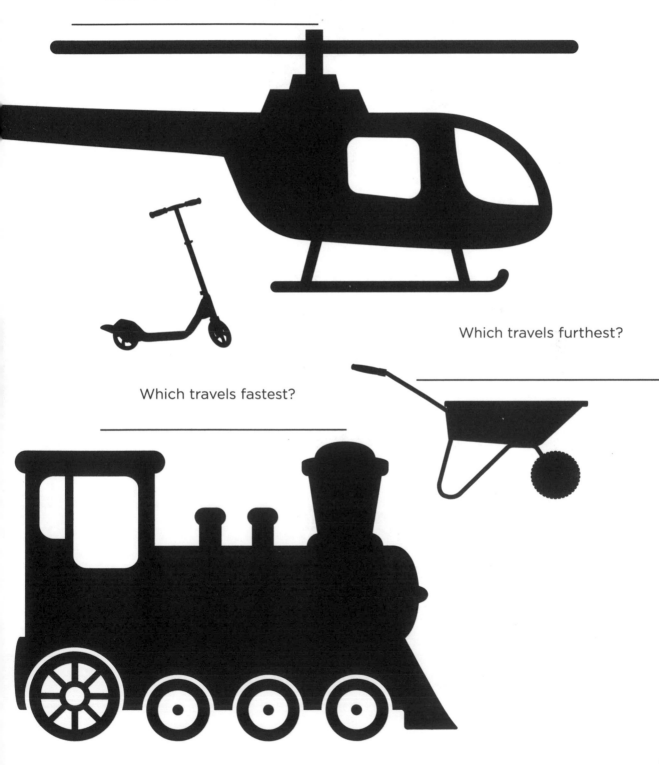

INVENT YOUR OWN VEHICLE

Things to think about:

How can you make it *fast*?

How can you make it *safe*?

How many people can it *fit*?

Who *won't be travelling* in it?

Why not?

What are you going to *call it*?

Where will you *go* in it?

IN THE MOOD

A Create a mood board for all your ideas.

Here are some thoughts
to get you started.

Idea one:

My Vehicle will have big wheels
that can also float on water.

TIME TO INVENT!

MY MARVELLOUS INVENTION

(Don't forget to label all its unique features.)

Gears are used in many machines that have moving parts, from watches to toys to bicycles. Each gear has teeth, or 'cogs', around the edges. When one gear turns, its cogs will fit into the next gear and turn it too. In this way, one small gear can make a big machine move!

Here are some rules for how gears work:

1. Each gear must touch the next gear to pass on the movement.

2. A clockwise gear (turning to the right) will turn the next gear anti-clockwise (turning to the left).

3. An anti-clockwise gear (turning to the left) will turn the next gear clockwise (turning to the right).

A If you turn each starting gear in the direction shown, which will get the bicycle rolling forwards? Circle your answer under each bike.

This bike will roll **FORWARDS** **BACKWARDS**

This bike will roll **FORWARDS** **BACKWARDS**

Speed is how fast an object moves. We measure speed by comparing the distance it travels with the time it takes to go that far.

So, the **average speed** is the distance travelled divided by the time it took.

The speed equation looks like this:

$$s = \frac{d}{t}$$

where d = the distance and t = the time.

a) Let's work out your average speed:

If you walk 10 kilometres to your friend's house (maybe think about catching a bus next time) and it takes you 5 hours, what is your average speed in kilometres per hour?

_____

_____

b) Let's work out your mum's average driving speed:

If your mum drives to work for 3 hours and she covers 180 kilometres, what is her average speed in kilometres per hour?

_____

_____

CHALLENGE

Can you work out average walking speeds for your family to see who is the *fastest* and who is the **s l o w e s t**?

You could design a Speed Chart like this:

Name	Walking Distance	Time it Took	Average Speed

Did you know?

The speed of **LIGHT** is the fastest speed in the universe. It is **299,792,458** metres per second.

The speed of **SOUND** is usually **343.2** metres per second

The speed of sound changes based on things like temperature and pressure.

Did you know this too?

GALILEO was the first scientist to measure speed as distance over time.

Sound travels much faster through something like water (about 1500 metres per second) because it is so much more dense.

TRAIN GAME

Trains can travel *fast*,
and they can travel s l o w .

Turn the page
to see the four
trains in
question!

Four trains all left the station
at different times.

Use the clues on the next page to figure
out the order in which they left, and then
number the trains from 1 to 4.

Train B is not last.

Train C left before Train D.

Train A didn't leave first.

**One train left between
Train B and Train D.**

Train A left after Train D.

TRAIN A

'Express' means fast but 'glaciers' are slow. This is called an oxymoron.

Slowest

The *Glacier Express* is one of the slowest express trains in the world.
It has to climb to the top of the Oberalp Pass in the Swiss Alps, travel across
291 bridges, go through 91 tunnels and cover 291 kilometres of track.
It takes about eight hours from start to finish.

TRAIN B

TRAIN C

_____

Fastest

The fastest train in the world is the *Shanghai Maglev* in China. It can travel at 460 kilometres per hour. Most trains use steel wheels on steel tracks but this speedster is the only passenger train in the world that uses magnetic levitation. That means it's travelling so fast it's literally flying!

TRAIN D

_____

PAPER

PLANES

It's time to make some paper planes so you can test how far you can fly them. Maybe ask a friend or your brother or sister to try this with you.

A paper plane doesn't have an engine like most aircraft, so it glides through the air using the force of your throw (called 'thrust') and the movement of air over and under the wings (which, when combined with the force of gravity, creates a phenomenon called 'lift' and this keeps the plane afloat). You'll need to fly your plane a few times and collect data so that you can compare each flight, which will be different.

·············· How to make a ··············

PAPER PLANE

WHAT DO YOU NEED?

A sheet of A4 paper

1. Fold your paper in half lengthways, then open it back up.

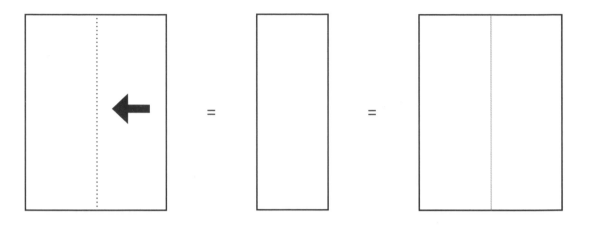

2. Fold the top corners inwards.

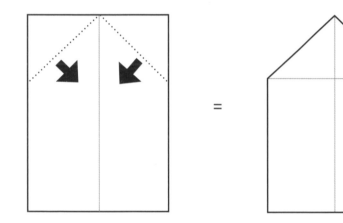

3. Fold the top corners in again.

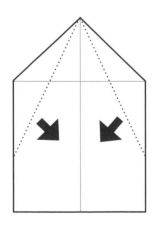
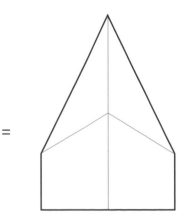

TIP:
If you build a plane launcher with an elastic band, this means that each plane can be launched in the same way and it might help you make more accurate measurements.

4. Fold in half.

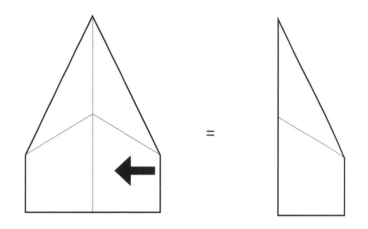

5. Fold down the wings.

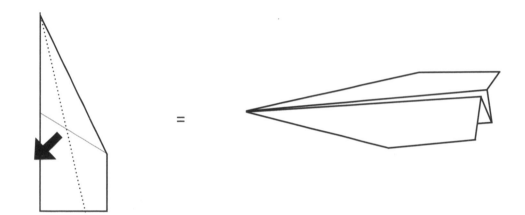

6. Time to fly!

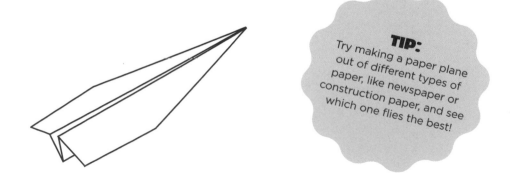

TIP:
Try making a paper plane out of different types of paper, like newspaper or construction paper, and see which one flies the best!

MY FLIGHT FINDINGS:

Flight 01:

Flight 02:

Flight 03:

MY FLIGHT FINDINGS:

Flight 04:

Flight 05:

Flight 06:

Design
YOUR OWN
PAPER PLANE

Design your own paper plane – folding it any way you like – to see if you can invent a design that travels even further.

Experiment with different designs and see what you discover.

MY FLIGHT FINDINGS:

Design 01:

Design 02:

Design 03:

It's usually much easier (and more fun!) to go downhill than uphill on a scooter or a bike. That's because gravity is doing most of the work instead of your legs.

Let's see what gravity will do to a marble. Can you control its fall by designing and building a path for the marble to follow?

·············· How to make a ··············

MARBLE RUN

WHAT DO YOU NEED?

Egg cartons

Glad wrap rolls

Masking tape

or toilet rolls

Instructions:

Check that this is okay with your parents first.

Tape your tubes with masking tape in different positions on a wall, a window or a glass door so that they form an obstacle course through which a marble can fall without stopping.

Can you design a marble run that takes exactly 30 seconds for the marble to complete?

YES

NO. *IMPOSSIBLE!*

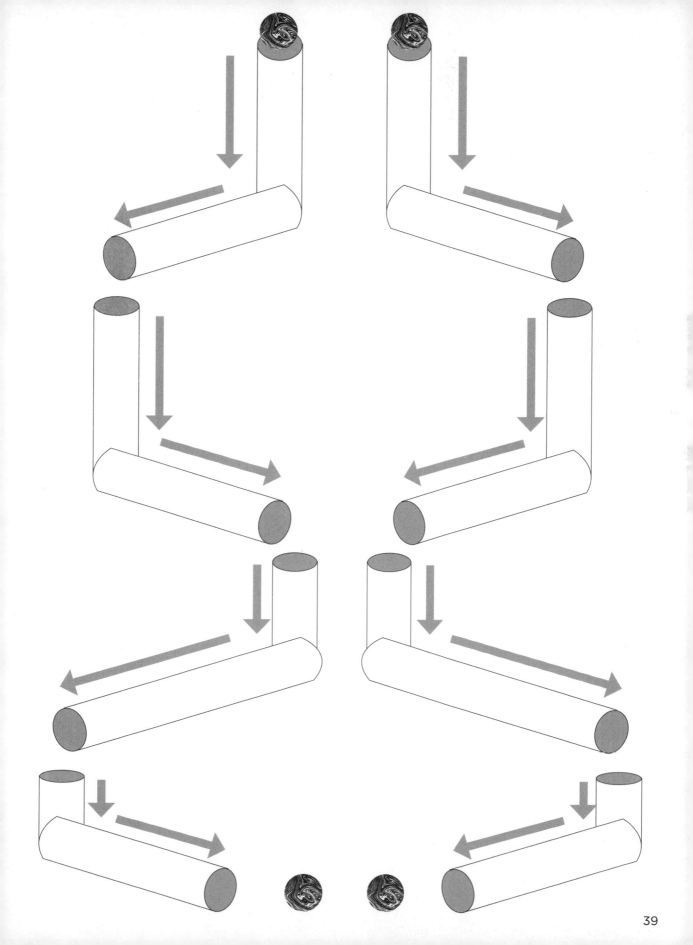

Science

Technology

Engineering

Maths

LOST IN SPACE

A rocket is lost and can't find its way home.

In space, no one can hear you scream!

A Can you provide directions for the shortest path to the planet?

PS: Watch out for all the space junk! (see page 44).

Move forward _____ spaces.

Turn _____.

Move forward _____ spaces.

Turn _____.

Move forward _____ spaces.

Turn _____.

Move forward _____ spaces.

Turn _____.

Move forward _____ spaces.

You have arrived!

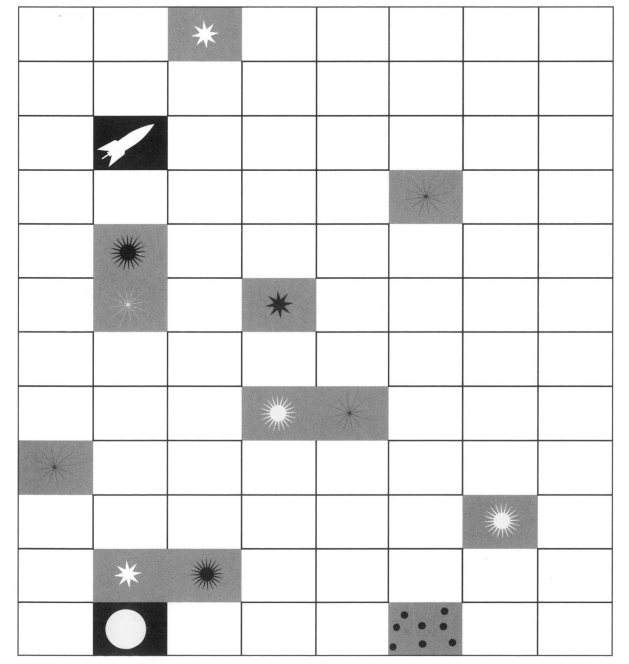

43

SPACE JUNK ALERT

There are about **2000** satellites orbiting around the Earth.

There are around **3000** old, not-working satellites orbiting around the Earth.

There are nearly **34,000** pieces of space junk bigger than the length of a pencil.

There are about **128 million** pieces of space junk as small as the tip of a pencil.

Can you navigate a path through all the space junk, ducking and diving along the way?

START HERE

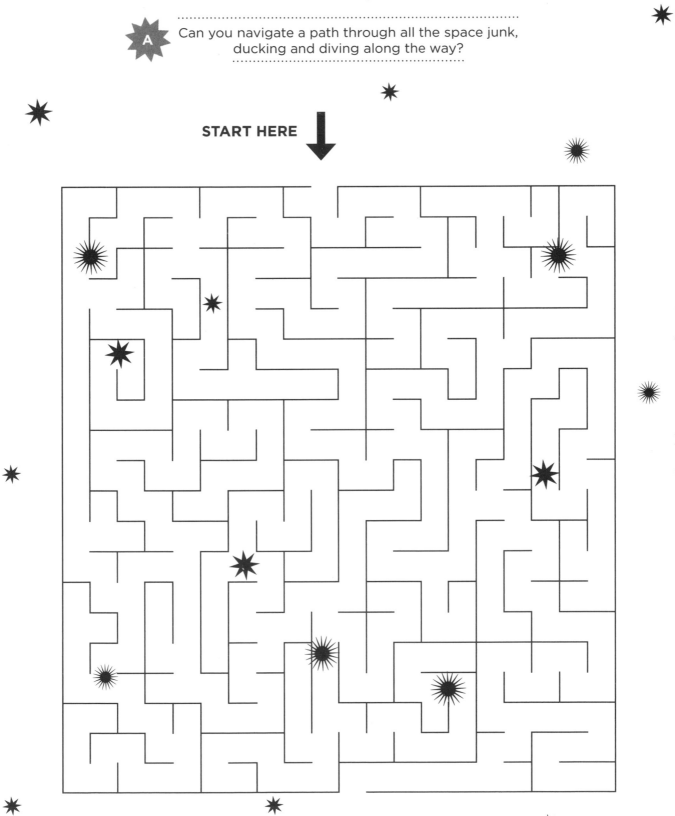

HOT

Space is **very, very cold** – way too cold for humans to go outside without *super-duper*, out-of-this world **warm clothes.**

What would you add to this spacesuit to help keep you warm?

Draw your ideas on this spacesuit.

COLD

Venus is **very**, **very hot** – the surface is around **450°C!**

What would you add to this spacesuit to help you stay cool?

Draw your ideas on this spacesuit.

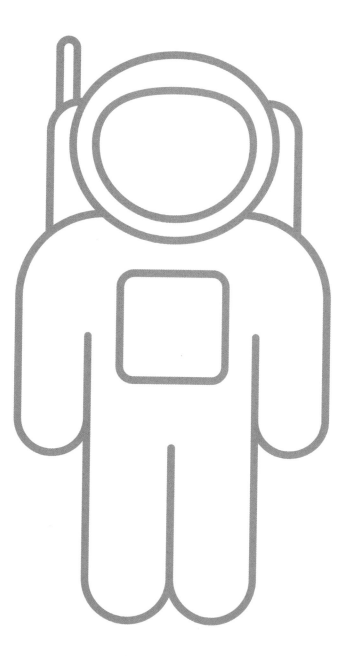

SPOT THE

These two spacecraft might look the same, but they're not.

Can you spot the 9 differences between the spacecraft?

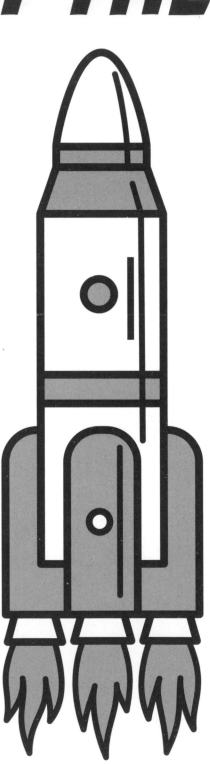

SPACECRAFT!

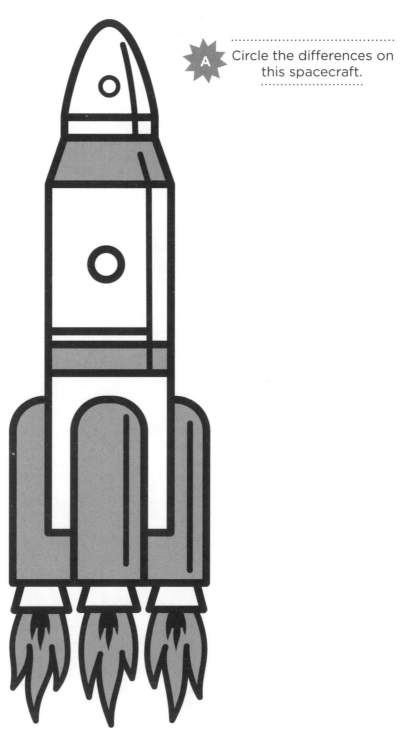

Circle the differences on this spacecraft.

COSMIC QUANTITIES

Space is **LARGE** – larger than we can ever really **IMAGINE**

(Although, imagination is like space: limitless).

BIG

Here are some really **BIG** facts about space.

1. Saturn has at least **145** moons, which is more than the rest of the planets in the solar system combined. (Earth only has one!)

2. There are more stars in the universe than grains of sand on Earth – more than **a billion trillion**.

3. You could fit around **1 million** Earths inside the Sun.

4. The largest asteroid in our solar system is named Ceres, and it is about **940** kilometres wide.

5. The Sun is **4.7 billion** years old, and will live for another 4 or 5 billion years.

6. The Milky Way galaxy, which is home to Earth, has more than **100 billion** stars.

7. The Sun is about **149.6 million** kilometres away from the Earth. This distance is called *1 Astronomical Unit*.

Can you put these facts in order from the smallest number
to the **biggest** number?

1. _____

2. _____

3. _____

4. _____

5. _____

6. _____

7. _____

There are eight planets in our solar system. We used to think there were nine planets, but Pluto was demoted when scientists discovered many other icy objects similar to Pluto in the same region of the solar system, which is now called the Kuiper Belt. Objects around Pluto's size are now called 'dwarf planets'.

ACROSS THE

4

3

2

1

A Name all the planets in order from the Sun as they stretch out across the universe.

7

6

5

8

UNIVERSE

SPACE QUIZ

How much do you know?

1. You can call me a gas giant. I am _____

2. I am definitely the biggest planet of them all. I am _____

3. My name rhymes with CARS. I am _____

4. I sizzle with heat. I am _____

5. I am freezing cold. I am _____

6. I have so many beautiful moons. I am _____

7. I am the first man on the moon. I am _____

8. I am the first dog in space. I am _____

9. I like to explode. I am a _____

10. I am the name of our galaxy. I am _____

TIME TO SHINE

Some stars die slowly. But really massive stars can go out in the **biggest bang possible**. This kind of star is called a **supernova** and, for just a moment, a supernova can be brighter than an entire galaxy.

Draw this super explosion! Make it as eye-catching as possible.

SEEING STARS

One of these stars is not like the others.

Can you spot which one?

ALIEN ART

The aliens in space are holding a drawing competition, but they need your help.

Your mission is to draw the other half of the alien portraits.

Each alien should be **symmetrical**: this means both halves should match.

THE PATTERNS

Science

Technology

Maths

AROUND US

Maths is everywhere we look!

It's in the leaves on the trees and in our DNA.

It's in the patterns on our footpaths and the shape of the stars.

It's in the thousands of raindrops in a rainbow.

These patterns can be hidden and not so easy to see so maths helps us discover them. It's not so easy for our eyes to see.

 Filll this page with as many spirals as possible.

Many patterns in nature reflect an important sequence called

The FIBONACCI SEQUENCE

Look closely at the sequence of numbers below:

0, 1, 1, 2, 3, 5, 8, 13, 21, 34, 55, 89

Can you see a pattern emerging?

Can you work out the next five numbers in this sequence?

YES ➡ Excellent. Go to page 196 to check your answers.

NO ➡ Good attempt. Check the tip below and try again, then go to page 196 to see the answer.

_____

_____

_____

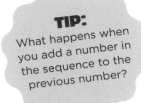

TIP:
What happens when you add a number in the sequence to the previous number?

_____

_____

Now, peer closely at a sunflower.

What can you see?

The seeds in the middle of a sunflower form spiral patterns that curve left and right.

If you count the number of spirals, your total will be a

FIBONACCI NUMBER.

How many spirals are in the sunflower above?

SHAPING UP

Shapes are all around us too:

squares

triangles

circles

rectangles

hexagons

spirals

octagons . . .

**They're in the buildings we can see,
the things we use, the food we eat,
the letters of the alphabet (see page 162) . . .**

Name the shapes below:

_____   _____   _____

_____   _____   _____

_____   _____   _____

_____   _____

FAVOURITE

FRACTALS

It's time to meet some of my favourite patterns of all:

FRACTALS

One type of fractal design is called **branching**.
To see branching at work:

1) Find a tree to stare at. It might be at home, in the playground or at school.

2) Look at the branches of trees and see how they grow out from the trunk.

3) Choose an answer that describes what you see.

    a) They get bigger and bigger as they get further away from the trunk.

    b) They get smaller and smaller as they get further away from the trunk.

    c) They become more and more tangled as they grow.

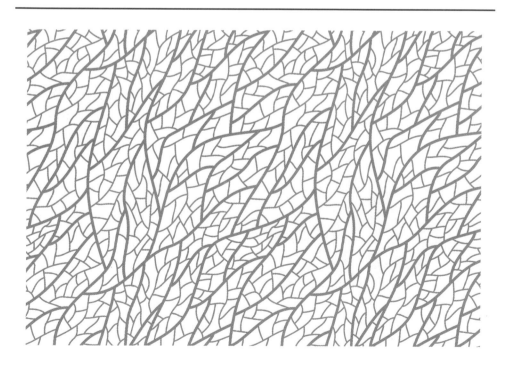

A branching fractal is a very efficient type of pattern because it allows oxygen and carbon dioxide to flow through the whole tree.

What else has a similar kind of pattern to the branches on the tree?

Circle the things that do.

LEAVES

SHOELACES

lightning

blood vessels

sunspots

CANDY FLOSS

ROCK FORMATIONS

rivers

Clue alert!

Colour this leaf while you think.

Did you know?

An average adult has around about 100,000 kilometres of blood vessels in their body. If you flew once around the world, you'd cover about 40,000 km. So the length of the blood vessels in your body is equivalent to flying around the world about two and a half times. WOW!

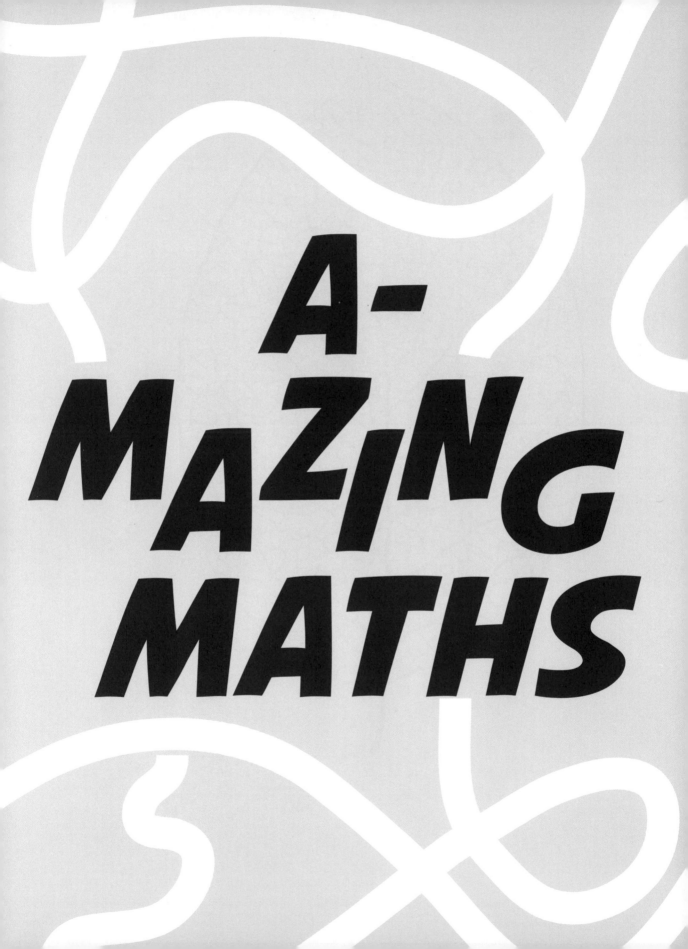

Starting at the top of this grid, find a path to the bottom (moving downwards or diagonally) that adds up to exactly 50.

2	13	5	8	3	6	4
8	1	7	6	4	5	9
11	4	3	1	8	7	1
9	5	8	2	9	10	6
7	2	4	9	1	4	2
1	6	10	5	7	9	8
6	8	9	4	2	3	12
5	4	1	3	8	5	7
3	2	8	9	6	1	3

ADDING UP

Can you cross out one number from each row so that each row and column add up to exactly 20?

7	1	5	4	3	2
6	4	7	2	1	6
5	6	1	4	2	3
2	4	2	5	7	5
3	5	3	7	4	2
3	2	3	3	7	4

BUILDING TRIANGLES

A Place the numbers 1–9 in these boxes so that each side of the triangle adds up to 20. I'll get you started with the number 8.

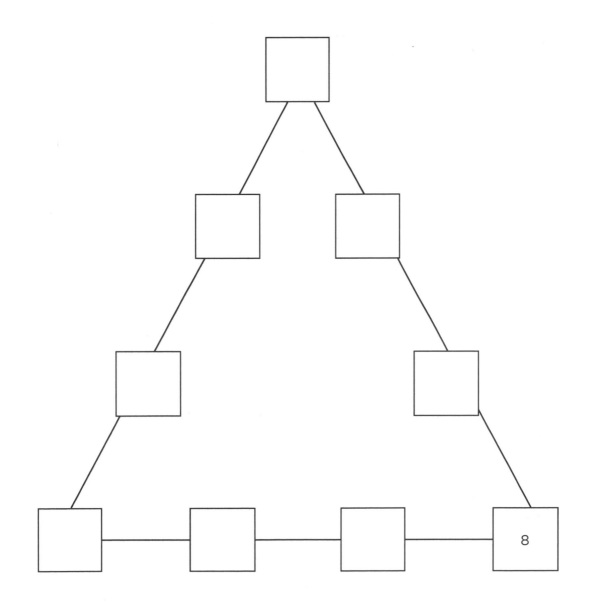

NUMBER CRUNCHING QUIZ

Some of the things on the next page are TRUE. And some of them ARE NOT.

Can you work out what's what?

Good luck!

		True	False

1. A pair of odd numbers always adds up to an odd number. _____

2. 10 x 4 + 39 - 62 = 16 (no calculators allowed!) _____

3. If you divided a pie into quarters and gave 75% of it to your best friend, you would have half left (YUM!) _____

4. 2100 hours is the same as 9 pm. _____

5. 3 is an odd number. _____

6. 3 is a prime number. _____

7. Maths is everywhere. _____

8. 2 is a prime number. _____

9. If you think of any two numbers, you can always find a number in between them. _____

+

**Add up all the numerals on this page.
Don't forget to include the page number.**

_____

I dream of eating ice cream every day of the year,

but I eat it only on special occasions.

On my birthday: **1**

After sports every Saturday: **52**

On the first day of every school term: **4**

On New Year's Eve AND New Year's Day: **2**

On International Ice Cream Day (3rd Sunday in July): **1**

How many ice creams do I eat in one year?

_____

How many ice creams will I have eaten by the time I am eighty?
(if I started eating them on the day I was born).

_____

Ask your friends and family about their ice cream habits!

ICE-CREAM SURVEY:

Name	Favourite flavour	No. of ice creams eaten

ICE-CREAM SURVEY: RESULTS

The biggest ice-cream eater I know is:

_____

The person with the most potential to eat more ice creams is:

_____

The flavour most people like is:

_____

The runner-up flavour is:

_____

SPAGHETTI SKYSCRAPER

I love spaghetti!

**Piled
high
with
TOMATO
SAUCE
and lots of
PARMESAN
CHEESE.**

But spaghetti might not be the first thing (or even second, third, fourth thing?) you think of as a building material.

In fact, you might be Very Surprised by just how versatile spaghetti can be.

Are you ready to take the spaghetti challenges to find out?

YES   **NO**

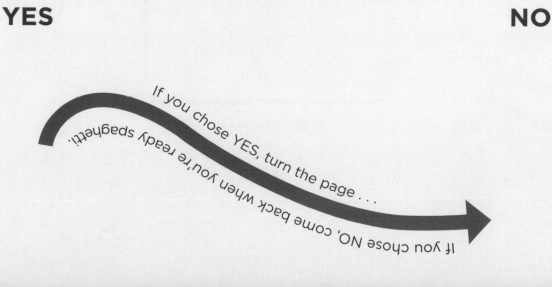

If you chose YES, turn the page . . .

If you chose NO, come back when you're ready spaghetti!

CHALLENGE NO. 1

Your challenge is to build the tallest structure you can with

30 PIECES of raw spaghetti,

1 METRE of sticky tape and

ONE marshmallow

WHAT DO YOU NEED?

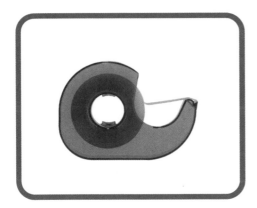

Sticky tape

Raw spaghetti

Marshmallow

WARNING: Do not eat the marshmallow before the tower is finished. You need to put it on the top of the tower – like a crown.

Instructions:

Figure out what your tower will look like.

Tips:

The Egyptians knew what they were doing when they built the pyramids many years ago. Think of a pyramid – which consists of triangles all the way around – as you build because triangles give a structure lots of strength.

Your tower should be broader at the base than at the top as this helps to distribute the weight.

You can break your spaghetti into smaller pieces if that helps, but they will need to be of equal length.

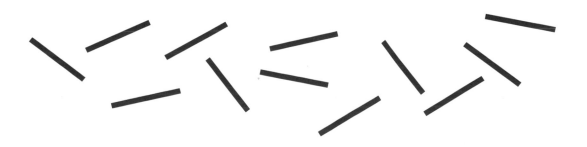

My spaghetti tower (draw it in the space above).

TWO **TALL** TOWERS

Eiffel Tower

This is on the Champs de Mars in Paris, France. It opened in 1889, stands at 300 metres, and was named after engineer Gustave Eiffel.

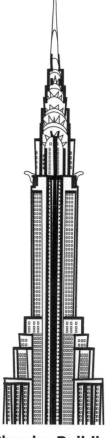

Chrysler Building

This is a skyscraper in New York City, United States. At 319 metres, it was the tallest building in the world – until the Empire State Building was built a year later.

CHALLENGE No. 2

Your next challenge is to build a 1-metre bridge from

250 G (HALF A PACK) of spaghetti and

5 METRES of sticky tape.

Instructions:

Look at some actual bridges first and then sketch a design.
It might look like this one:

Tip:

Triangles are often used in bridges too.

What can your bridge support?	*Yes*	*You've got to be kidding!*
Me		
My lunchbox		
My little brother/sister		
A can of corn		
My mum/dad		
My left leg		

Congratulations!
The wearer of this badge is a

RHYME TIME

What rhymes with SPAGHETTI?

confetti   yeti   Betty   sweaty   jetty   petty   settee   Eddie

A Write a squiggly spaghetti poem using some of these words.

_____

_____

_____

_____

_____

_____

ODD PASTA OUT

A Circle all the non-pasta things on the opposite page.

Science

Technology

Engineering

Maths

Making a pinwheel is a great way to see force and motion,
cause and effect in action.

PIN-WHEEL

WHAT DO YOU NEED?

A pair of scissors

A pencil

A ruler

A pin

A square piece of paper

A straw

Masking tape

Instructions:

1. Mark the centre of your paper with the pencil.

2. Draw a diagonal line with your ruler from each corner of the paper, halfway to your dot.

3. Cut along the diagonal lines you have drawn.

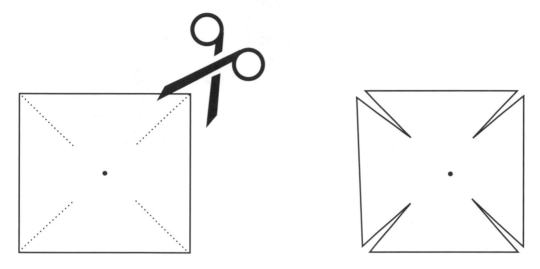

4. Fold every other point into the centre dot and fix the paper with a pin.

5. Hold your straw behind the paper and push the rest of the pin through the straw, to create a handle.

6. Cover the end of the pin with some masking tape so you don't prick yourself.

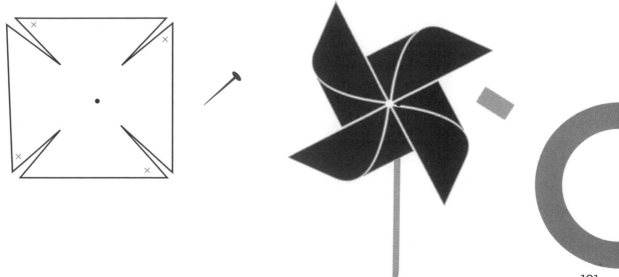

A Use a hairdryer (or your breath) to blow into your pinwheel and record how many revolutions it makes in 1 minute.

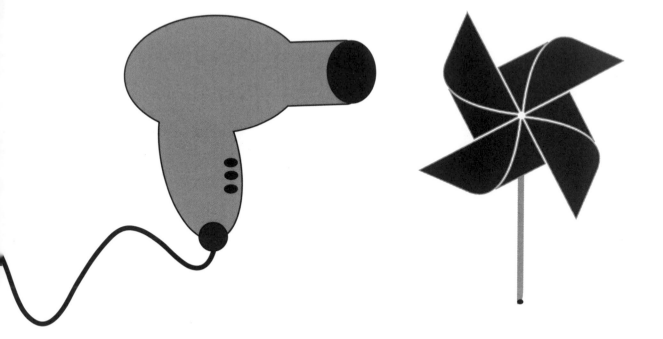

Spin Records

Recorded by _____

Date _____

Time _____

Observations _____

_____

_____

_____

Pinwheel designs are great at spinning, so they are used as turbines to capture the wind and generate power.

Measuring the wind

You can measure the wind by its speed and direction.

An anemometer is a special type of instrument that measures wind speed. There are many different types of anemometers but some have a spinning wheel. The stronger the wind blows, the faster the wheel rotates. The anemometer counts the number of rotations, which is then used to work out the wind speed.

Weather vanes or wind vanes measure the direction of the wind.

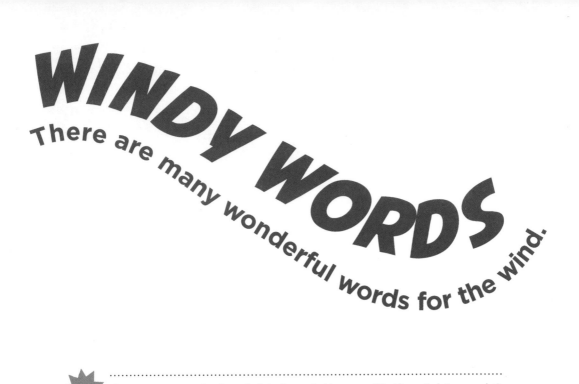

WINDY WORDS

There are many wonderful words for the wind.

A Can you match the right descriptions with the right words?

PS: You might need to do some research. Or not. You might be a wind expert already.

SIROCCO

A whirly, twirly Australian wind that whisks up dust devils.

Zephyr

A gentle breeze.

Gale

This wind howls across the moors.

Aeolian

These winds shape the surface of the earth and create things like sand dunes.

SQUALL

SOUTHERLY BUSTER

A cold wind that blows over the Mediterranean coast.

Brickfielder

A hot, dry wind that blows from the Sahara Desert into Africa and Italy.

Wuther

Haboob

A hot and dry Australian wind.

MISTRAL

This can whip up a sandstorm.

A stormy wind that can bring rain or snow.

WILLIWAW

Willy-willy

This sudden, cool wind comes, unsurprisingly, from the south.

Brrr. This is a stormy cold wind that blasts down mountainsides.

This is a strong, fast-moving wind. Hold on to your hat!

DRAWING THE WIND

Read the descriptions of the different winds again and then draw how you think some of them might look in these boxes.

We can't see the wind – we can only feel and imagine it – so there is no right or wrong.

Here's one of my drawings:

Willy-willy

CLOUD GUIDE

There are many different types of clouds.

Here are the Top Ten

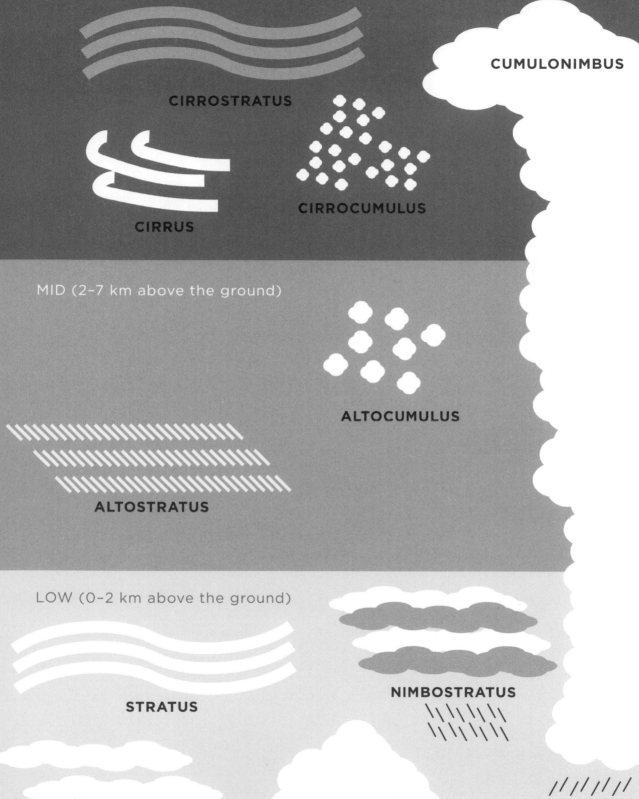

HIGH (5–13 km above the ground)

CIRROSTRATUS

CIRRUS

CIRROCUMULUS

CUMULONIMBUS

MID (2–7 km above the ground)

ALTOCUMULUS

ALTOSTRATUS

LOW (0–2 km above the ground)

STRATUS

NIMBOSTRATUS

STRATOCUMULUS

CUMULUS

CLOUDY DAYS AHEAD

What clouds do you see this week?

MONDAY

TUESDAY

WEDNESDAY

THURSDAY

FRIDAY

SATURDAY

SUNDAY

CLOUD WORD SEARCH

A Can you find these cloudy words in the word search?

becloud	thundercloud	cloudiness
cloudless	cloudlet	clouds
cloudy	cloudberries	cloudscapes

```
C  M  N  B  V  C  X  Z  L  C  T  A  S  D  F  G
L  J  K  L  O  I  U  Y  T  L  H  R  E  W  C  Q
O  A  S  D  F  Z  B  F  Q  O  U  Z  D  F  L  H
U  D  B  E  C  L  O  U  D  U  N  G  L  W  O  P
D  Q  W  T  A  J  K  Z  C  D  D  A  T  P  U  A
I  G  S  Q  G  H  Z  D  F  S  E  X  S  C  D  V
N  M  B  V  C  X  Z  A  S  C  R  Q  D  W  L  A
E  A  S  D  F  G  H  J  K  A  C  L  U  M  E  N
S  E  W  Q  D  A  Y  Z  X  P  L  C  O  V  S  B
S  R  T  Y  U  D  I  O  P  E  O  L  L  K  S  Z
B  G  H  M  U  K  L  I  U  S  U  T  C  R  E  Q
V  J  D  O  A  L  S  G  T  F  D  H  E  L  Q  T
W  E  L  Y  P  Y  A  O  V  G  Q  U  S  R  E  W
Q  C  I  C  L  O  U  D  B  E  R  R  I  E  S  H
Z  A  H  U  Q  S  H  R  K  I  S  M  N  D  F  I
H  C  O  C  L  O  U  D  L  E  T  I  U  Y  T  R
```

BEYOND THE THUNDERCLOUD

Did you know you can make **590 word**s from the word

THUNDERCLOUD?

WOW!

 Can you find just 10 words? (Easy peasy!)

1.

2.

3.

4.

5.

6.

7.

8.

9.

10.

Look at the word cloud below.

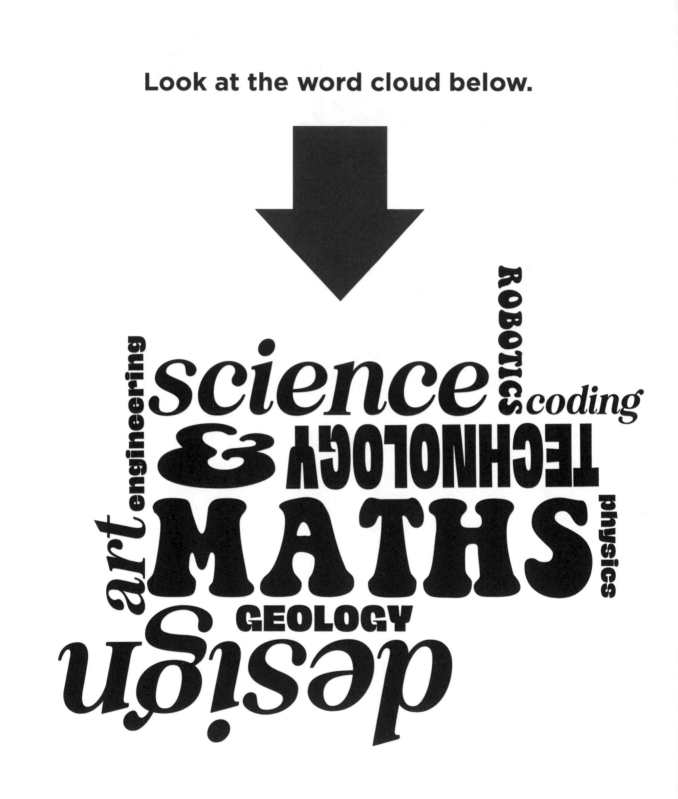

1. Work out what you want to say in your cloud.

2. Think about the shape you want for your cloud.

3. Create your cloud.

My Word Cloud

CLOUD SPOTTING

The study of clouds is called

nephology.

This word comes from the Greek word **nephos**, which means **kidney**, because clouds resemble kidneys (*sort of*).

Most people have two kidneys:

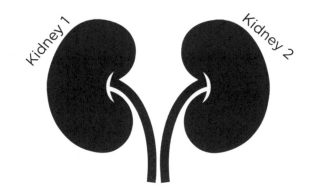

Kidney 1

Kidney 2

Your two kidneys sit side by side just below your ribcage, on either side of your spine. They are about the size of your fist, and have the very important job of filtering out waste from your blood and turning it into urine.

Together, they filter **200** litres of fluid every 24 hours.

1. How many litres is that every week?

_____

_____

2. How many weeks are there in a year?

_____

_____

3. How many litres do the kidneys filter every year?

You might need a calculator for some of these tough questions!

_____

_____

4. How many litres have *your* kidneys filtered? (Hint: How many years have you been alive?)

_____

_____

5. How many litres do the kidneys in your family filter every week?

_____

_____

Have you ever thought about how a boat can float, even when it's made out of metal? It's because of something called buoyancy: water pushes up while the boat pushes water down and away. It's also because of density: if a boat is too heavy for its size, it will sink.

Boats made out of aluminium foil are surprisingly watertight. If you don't believe me, you can test this out yourself.

·············· How to make a ··············

(watertight)
BOAT

WHAT DO YOU NEED?

Aluminium foil

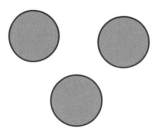

A few coins

A bucket, a basin, or a bathtub filled with water

A ruler

1. Cut out a square sheet of foil that is 30 cm long on each side, using a ruler to measure.

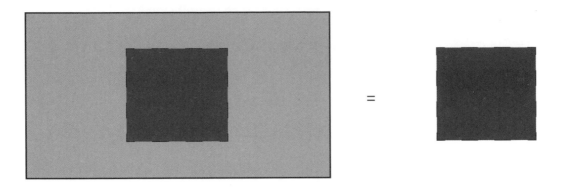

2. Now fold up the sides to make the shape of a boat and see how it floats on water.

3. Try putting small coins into the boat to see how much weight it can support before it sinks.

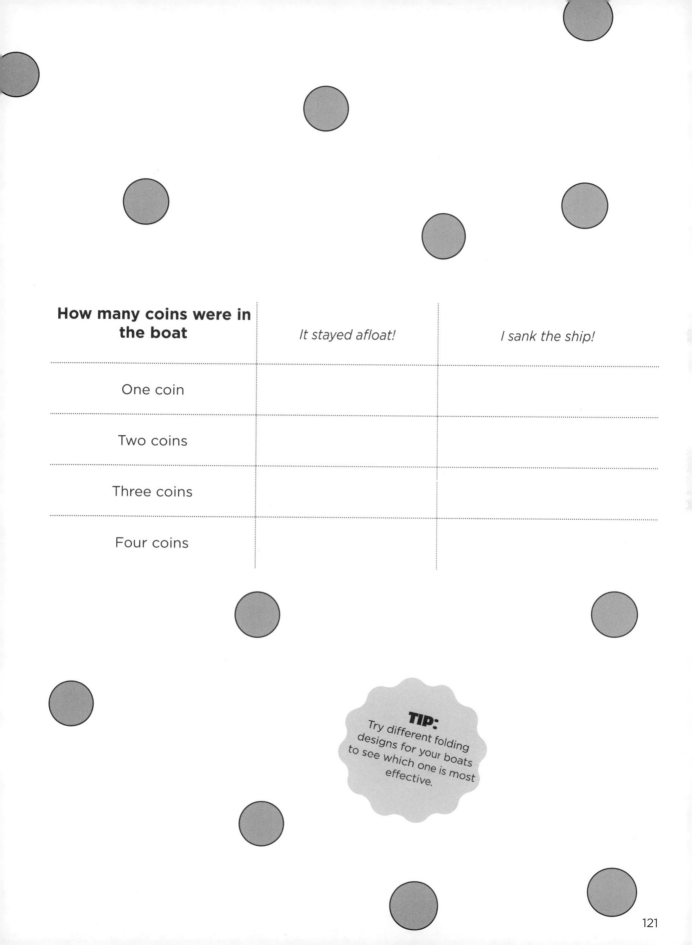

How many coins were in the boat	It stayed afloat!	I sank the ship!
One coin		
Two coins		
Three coins		
Four coins		

TIP:
Try different folding designs for your boats to see which one is most effective.

Science

Engineering

ROBO +

In 1942, science-fiction author Isaac Asimov wrote three rules for robots.

The rules are:

1. First Law

A robot may not injure a human being or allow a human being to come to harm by not doing anything.

2. Second Law

A robot must obey the orders given it by human beings except where such orders would conflict with the First Law.

3. Third Law

A robot must protect its own existence as long as such protection does not conflict with the First or Second Law.

MY ROBOT LAWS

By _____

LAW ONE: _____

_____

_____

_____

LAW TWO: _____

_____

_____

_____

LAW THREE: _____

_____

_____

_____

A Draw your own robot using ONLY squares.

How many squares can you find in this picture?

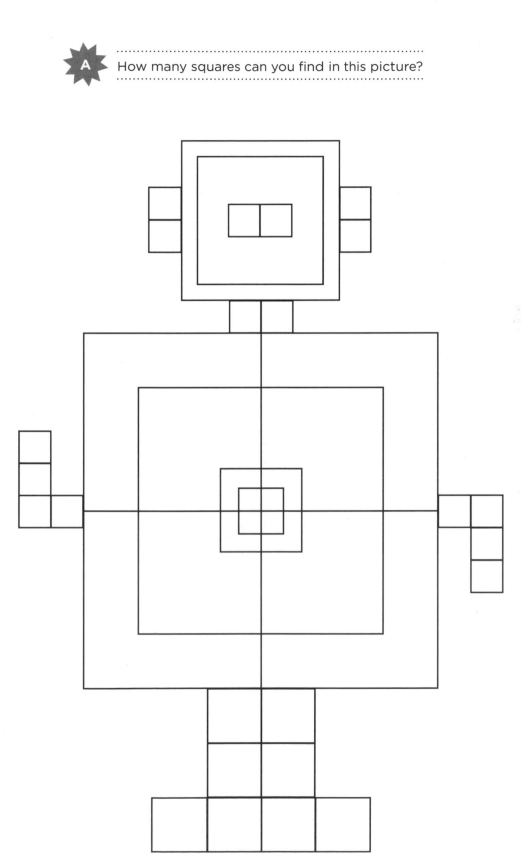

Hint: They might be big. They might be small.

129

Drones are an important piece of

MODERN TECHNOLOGY.

They can *fly high* and **far,** and they often travel to places that are too dangerous or difficult for people to reach. They can be small enough to fit in your hand or as big as a plane. Some drones can take videos, or even carry packages.

Because drones don't have pilots, they are usually flown by remote control or by running a program that tells them where to go and what to do.

Drones can be used to:

☞ Take photos or videos from the air

☞ Deliver food and supplies

☞ Monitor traffic

☞ Make maps of remote places.

Did you know?

Drones are named after a type of honey bee.

These drones are delivering packages to different people.

 Draw a line from each drone to its destination.

133

AHOY, TREASURE BELOW

There are ten pieces of treasure hidden somewhere on this map.

Can you help a drone find all the treasure from the sky by marking the map, following the coordinates below?

The first one is found for you.

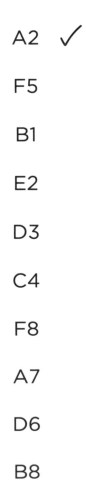

A2 ✓

F5

B1

E2

D3

C4

F8

A7

D6

B8

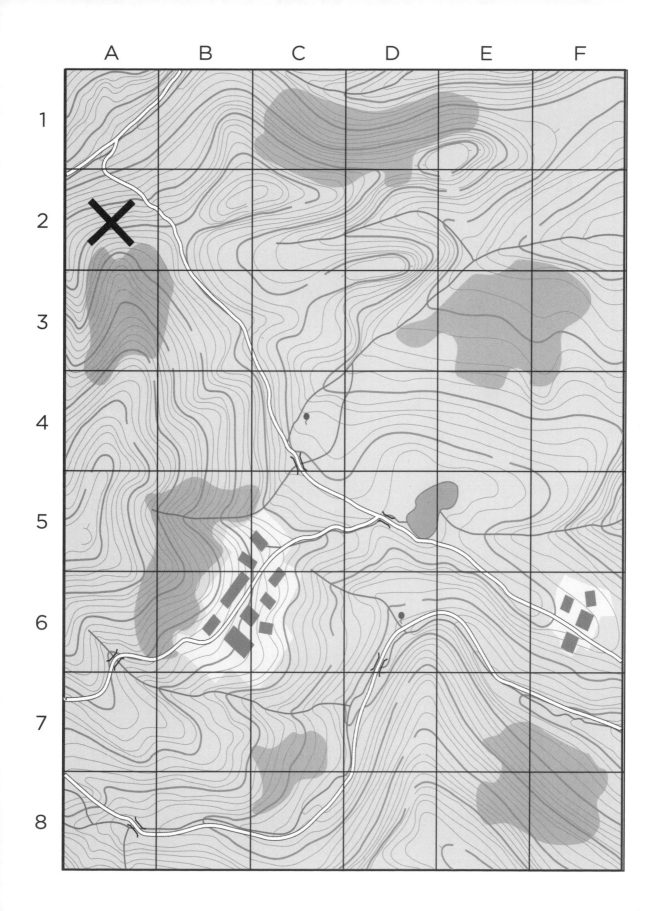

Once you've located all ten pieces, create a path for the drone that lets it visit all the treasure, starting at any piece of treasure and moving square by square (no diagonals!).

What's the smallest number of squares the drone will need to travel through to see all ten pieces of treasure?

Use the map on the next page to test out different routes. Use the space below to record your attempts.

STARTING COORDINATE	ENDING COORDINATE	NUMBER OF SQUARES

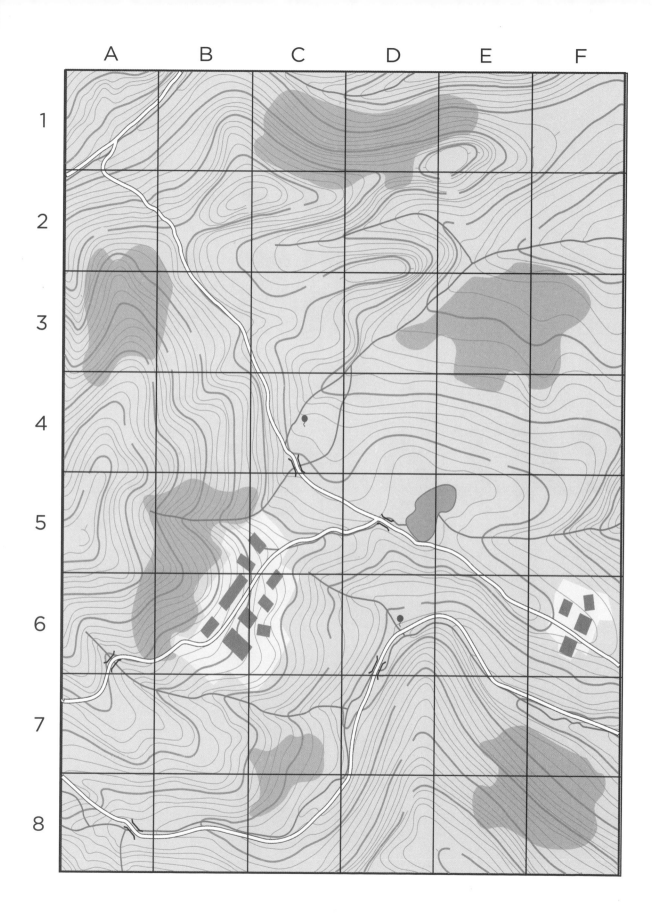

When we build robots, they need to be able to stand up and move around on their own. To do this, they need to be able to balance. The balance of an object has everything to do with the distribution of mass in it.

WHAT DO YOU NEED?

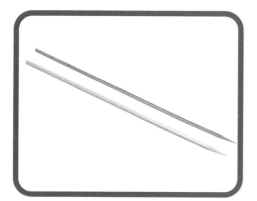

Skewers

Marshmallows
(hope you have a big bag!)

Instructions:

Slide three marshmallows onto the ends of a skewer.
Place one marshmallow in the middle, and one at each end.

Put your finger under the middle marshmallow and try
to balance it on your finger. Can you do it?

If not, adjust the marshmallow in the middle a little to the left or right,
until you reach the point where you can balance it on your finger.
This is called the **Original Balance Point**.

But what happens if you add more marshmallows on one side?
Where does the balance point move to?

Try adding more skewers (connected with marshmallows) and see how you
can change the centre of gravity (balance point) for the whole skewer system.

CHAIN REACTION

Robots and drones are complex systems that rely on many interconnected parts. This activity shows you how small parts can work together to create a very big reaction.

This is a great activity to do with friends. The aim is to create a long chain by weaving popsicle sticks together.

Once you've worked it out, you can make your chain longer and longer. Or shorter and shorter to see what kind of difference this makes.

WHAT DO YOU NEED?

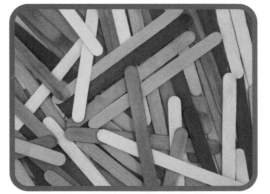

A large bag of coloured popsicle sticks

Instructions:

1. Make an X shape with the first two popsicle sticks.

2. As you add sticks, make sure the new stick always goes over one stick and under the other (so you are bending and pinning the sticks, which creates tension). Always hold down the X shape you are building onto to keep the tension going. Ask a friend to help if you need to.

3. Keep building the chain for as long as you can, or until you run out of sticks.

4. Release your hold on the chain and STAND BACK as the tension is released and popsicle sticks fly through the air!

CONGRATULATIONS

You have just converted **potential energy** into **kinetic energy.**

That's the energy something has when it's in motion.

Art & design are an important
part of everything we do.

Art helps us understand the world
and allows us to express what we see and
how we feel in a playful way.

Design is how we solve prolems
in creative ways.

Design and art are FUN ways we can
look at the world around us.

THE BEAUTY OF SYMMETRY

One of the most amazing things in this world is the beauty
of natural symmetry.

This is when something in nature, like a butterfly's wings, a flower,
or even your body, is made up of two or more identical,
or very similar, parts.

It's nature's artwork!

In your garden or at the park, how many things can you find that are
symmetrical? Draw them on the opposite page.

MY SMALL SYMMETRICAL FINDS

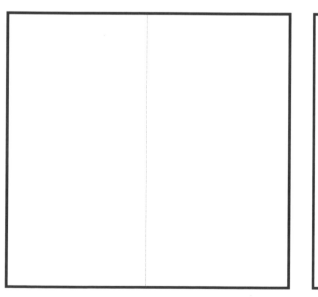

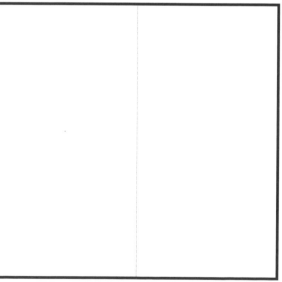

MY BIG SYMMETRICAL FINDS

A Make your own symmetrical butterfly

Using paint, create a single butterfly wing.

Before it dries, carefully turn this page over,
so the wing imprints onto the other page.

Open the pages back up, and leave them out to dry.

And admire your beautiful, symmetrical butterfly!

Paint your wing on this side.

NATURE'S PAINT-BRUSHES

The shapes and patterns you find in nature can make the most extraordinary paintbrushes.

What amazing paintbrushes can you find in your garden or local park? Dip your objects in some paint and use the page opposite to show your beautiful findings.

Experiment with your nature brushes here.

FRUIT SALAD MYSTERY

I chopped up some fruit for my breakfast and decided
to turn them into prints.

A Can you guess which fruits I ate?

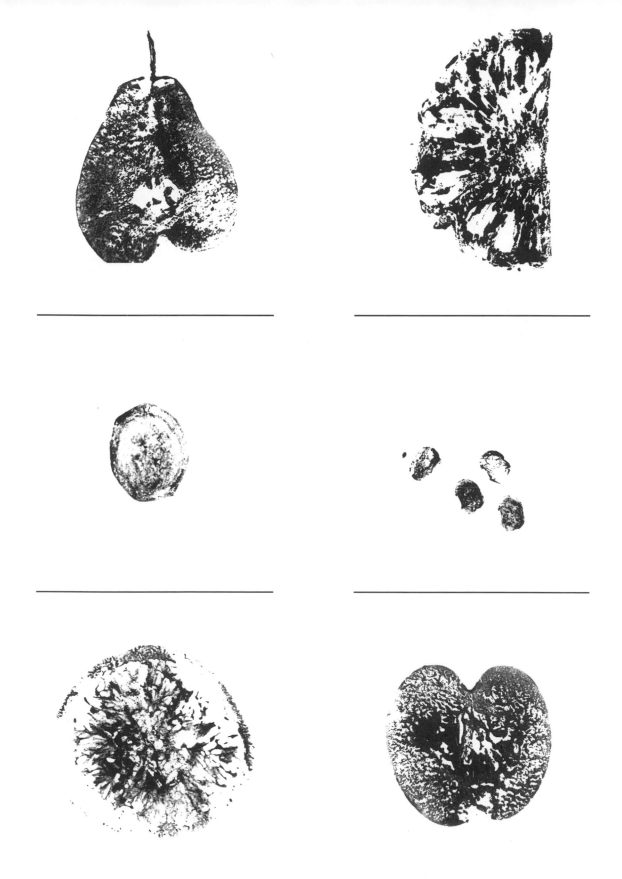

How to make

NATURE FRIENDS

WHAT DO YOU NEED?

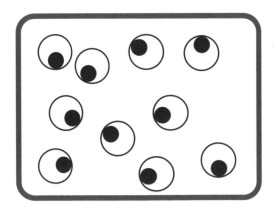

I-Spy eyes

Glue

Instructions:

Collect some random nature objects with interesting shapes.
These might be rocks, leaves, pieces of bark or even flowers.

Once you've collected a few, take them home and wipe them with
a wet rag (clean all that extra dirt off!).

Using the glue, stick two eyes onto each object and VOILA!
You've made some new friends.

Place them around the home or in your bedroom for everyone to meet!

Colour in this field of flowers.

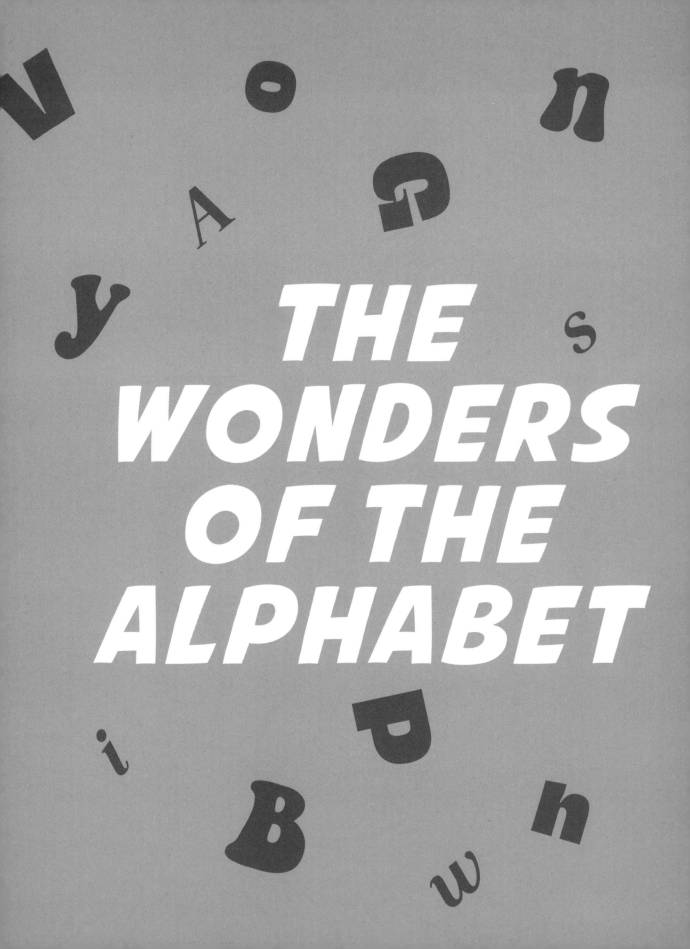

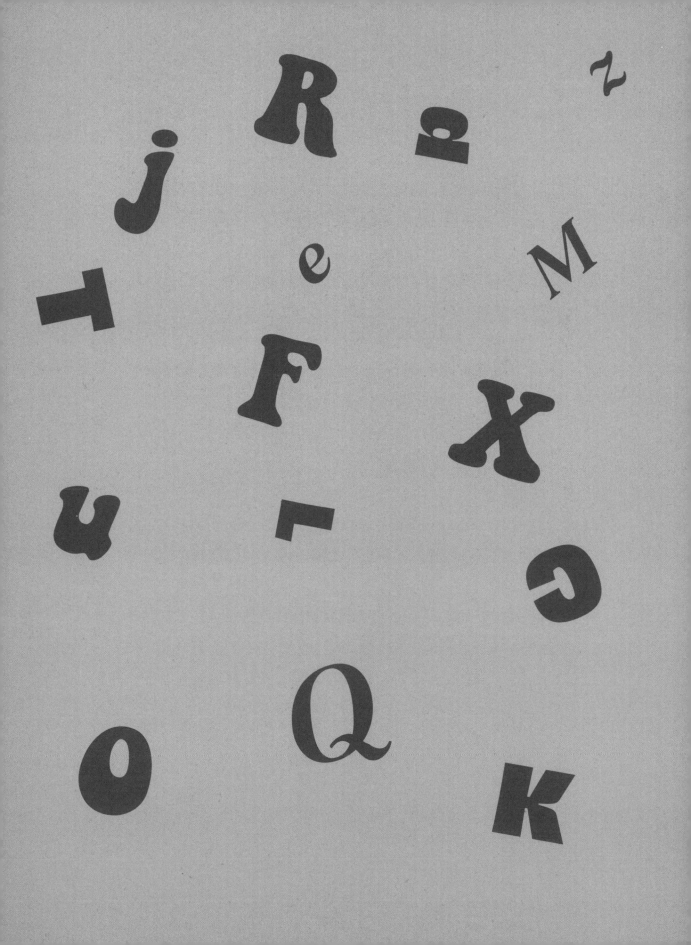

We are surrounded by words
and letters EVERY DAY.

They're everywhere.

In books, on signs, on phones,
on TVs, on the tags of our clothes,
on cereal boxes . . .

But have you ever stopped to think about
what letters ACTUALLY look like?

The art of designing letters is called
TYPOGRAPHY. Designing letters
is a very important job.

Letters of the alphabet are made up of some key shapes:

CIRCLES

SQUARES

RECTANGLES

TRIANGLES

How many shapes can you see in this alphabet below? Use a pencil to colour them in. I've done the first three for you.

J K L M N

S T U V

E F G H I

O P Q R

W X Y Z

DESIGN YOUR OWN font

Using shapes, can you design each letter of the alphabet to create your own FONT?

Don't forget to give it a *cool* name once you've finished!

The shapes

Use the space below to sketch some ideas before laying out your font on the next page

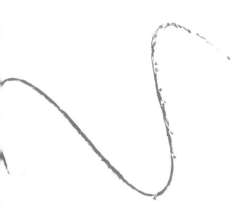

My font:

A   B   C   D

J   K   L   M   N

S   T   U   V

My font name: _____

E   F   G   H   I

O   P   Q   R

W   X   Y   Z

Write some messages to friends using your new font.

Psst: Don't forget to give them your font so they can decipher the messages.

TO:

TOP-SECRET MESSAGE

FROM:

TO:

TOP-SECRET MESSAGE

FROM:

LettErs make up THE WORLD

Letters make up WORDS.

WORDS make SENTENCES.

SENTENCES make STORIES.

STORIES make BOOKS.

BOOKS are ALL AROUND US!

Do you have a story you'd like to tell?
Or maybe one you've already written?

Well, together let's make a book, and you can fill that
book with a story, or anything you like.

A BOOK

WHAT DO YOU NEED?

1 x A4 sheet of paper

A pair of scissors

1. Fold your paper in half.

=

2. Turn the folded page 90°, and fold your paper in half again.

3. Turn the folded page 90° again, and fold your paper in half once more.

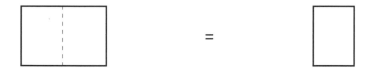

4. Unfold the paper twice so it's still folded once in half. You'll be able to see the fold marks across the middle.

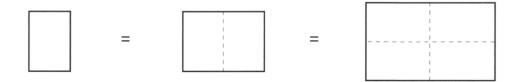

5. Holding the paper horizontally so the fold is on the bottom, carefully cut along the middle fold up to the centre.

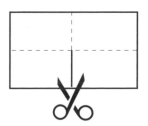

6. Unfold the paper completely. There will now be a slit down the very middle of the page.

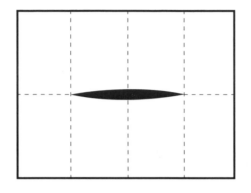

7. Fold the paper in half again, this time lengthwise.

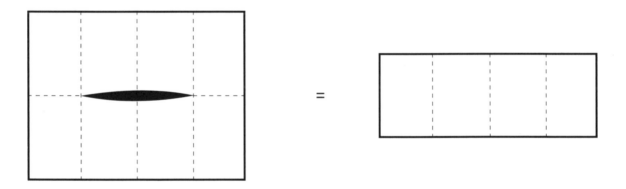

8. Hold up the folded page, and fold the page in on itself, creating a four pointed star shape from the cut out gap .

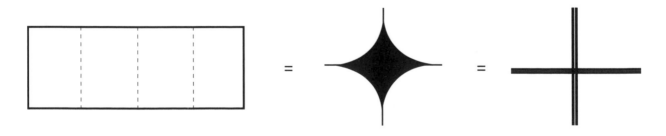

9. Now fold down the arms of the star shape to make a small rectangle.

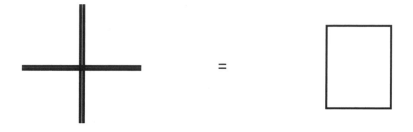

10. Now you have an 8-page booklet you can use for your story, your drawings, or anything you like. Don't forget to leave the front blank so you can design your book cover.

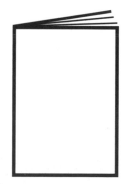

Design your book cover

Now that your book is ready, it's time to give it a face!

Let's design a book cover.

Before you start, you need to brainstorm
some ideas to draw from as inspiration.

Write down ideas for your cover. I've left some prompts there
if you're stuck.

Once you've come up with key images, you can choose what
kind of lettering to use for the title and author name.
Maybe you can use the font you designed earlier.

There are two covers on the next page for you to try out
your ideas before you do your final cover.

Have fun!

BRAINSTORMING

Is there a main character? What do they look like?

What kind of ending does the story have?
Happy or sad?

What colours can you see in your book?

Where does the story take place?

Maybe this is a story without words.
Pictures tell stories too.

DRAFT COVER ONE

DRAFT COVER TWO

ANSWERS

(DON'T PEEK!)

ACRONYM ALERT

RADAR	**Radio Detection And Ranging**
SCUBA	**Self-Contained Underwater Breathing Apparatus**
DNA	**Deoxyribonucleic Acid**
BASIC	**Beginner's All-purpose Symbolic Instruction Code**
LASER	**Light Amplification by Stimulated Emission of Radiation**
LED	**Light Emitting Diode**
ET	**Extraterrestrial**
ROYGBIV	**Red, Orange, Yellow, Green, Blue, Indigo, Violet**
NASA	**National Aeronautics and Space Administration**
ASAP	**As Soon As Possible**
BRB	**Be Right Back**
PDF	**Portable Document Format**
FOMO	**Fear Of Missing Out**
RAM	**Random Access Memory**

Page 10-11:

Which was invented first? **The wheelbarrow**

Which was invented last? **The rocket (as a vehicle for people – explosive rockets have been around a long time)**

Which travels fastest? **The rocket**

Which travels furthest? **The rocket**

Which is the safest? **Depends! The more complicated a vehicle is, the higher the potential danger.**

Page 18-19:

Bike one will roll **FORWARDS**

Bike two will roll **BACKWARDS**

Page 21:

a) **2 km per hr**

b) **60 km per hr**

Page 26-27:

The trains left in this order: **B, C, D and A**

Page 42-43:

Move forwards **2** spaces.

Turn **right**.

Move forward **7** spaces.

Turn **left**.

Move forward **1** spaces.

Turn **right**.

Move forward **2** spaces.

Turn **right**.

Move forward **2** spaces.

You have arrived!

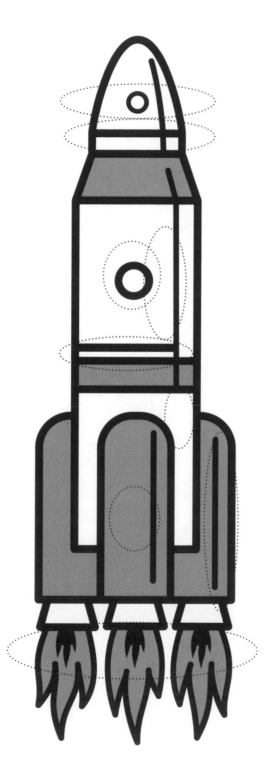

Page 51:

1. Saturn has at least **145** moons, which is more than the rest of the planets in the solar system combined. (Earth only has one!)

2. The largest asteroid in our solar system is named Ceres, and it is about **940** km wide.

3. You could fit around **1 million** Earths inside the Sun.

4. The Sun is about **149.6 million** km away from the Earth. This distance is called *1 Astronomical Unit.*

5. The Sun is **4.7 billion** years old, and will live for another 4 or 5 million years.

6. The Milky Way galaxy, which is home to Earth, has over **100 billion** stars.

7. There are more stars in the universe than grains of sand on Earth – more than **a billion trillion.**

Page 52-53:

The planets in order from the sun are:

1. Mercury

2. Venus

3. Earth

4. Mars

5. Jupiter

6. Saturn

7. Uranus

8. Neptune

Page 54:

1. You can call me a gas giant. I am (*this is a trick question because there are four gas giants so the answer can be any of these. Or all of them*) either **Jupiter**, **Saturn**, **Uranus** or **Neptune**.

2. I am definitely the biggest planet of them all. I am **Jupiter**.

3. My name rhymes with CARS. I am **Mars**.

4. I sizzle with heat. I am **Venus**.

5. I am freezing cold. I am **Uranus**.

6. I have the most moons of all. I am **Saturn.**

7. I am the first man on the moon. I am **Neil Armstrong**.

8. I am the first dog in space. I am **Laika**.

9. I like to explode. I am a **supernova**.

10. I am the name of our galaxy. I am **The Milky Way**.

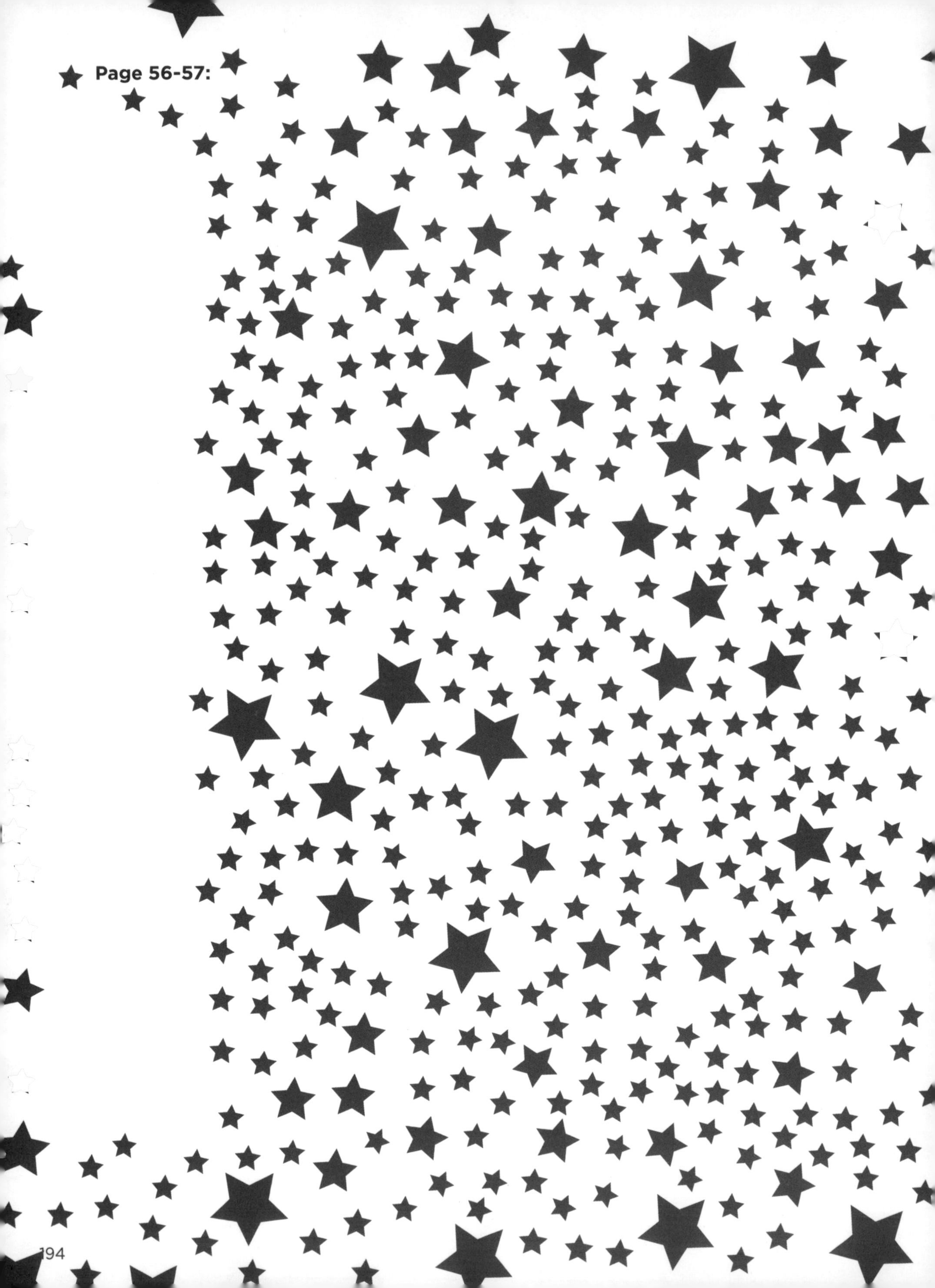

Page 67:

144

233

377

610

987

Page 69: 13

Page 71:

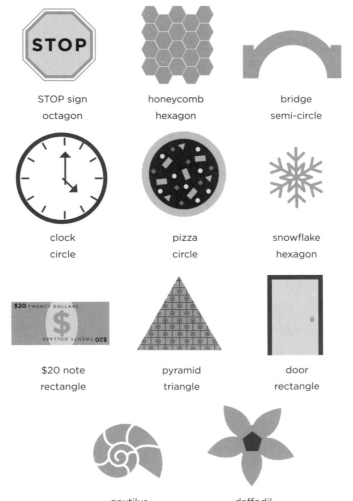

STOP sign
octagon

honeycomb
hexagon

bridge
semi-circle

clock
circle

pizza
circle

snowflake
hexagon

$20 note
rectangle

pyramid
triangle

door
rectangle

nautilus
spiral

daffodil
pentagon (or star)

b) They get smaller and smaller as they get further away from the trunk.

Page 74:

Page 77:

2	13	5	8	3	(6)	4
8	1	7	6	4	(5)	9
11	4	3	1	(8)	7	1
9	5	8	(2)	9	10	6
7	2	4	(9)	1	4	2
1	6	10	5	(7)	9	8
6	8	9	(4)	2	3	12
5	4	(1)	3	8	5	7
3	2	(8)	9	6	1	3

Page 78:

7	1	5	4	3	⊗
⊗	4	7	2	1	6
5	6	⊗	4	2	3
2	4	2	⊗	7	5
3	5	3	7	⊗	2
3	⊗	3	3	7	4

Page 79:

Example answer – other answers are possible.

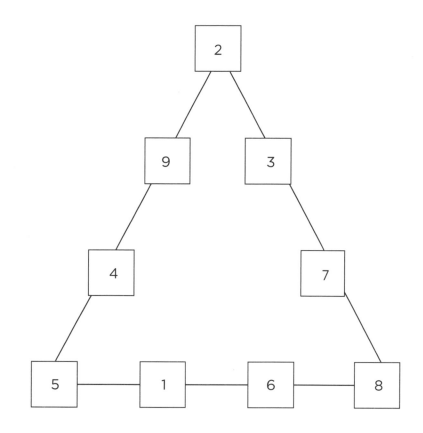

Page 81:

1. A pair of odd numbers always add up to an odd number.

F. They add up to an even number. I know. That sounds odd!

2. 10 x 4 + 39 - 62 = 16

F. The answer is 17 (so close!)

3. If you divided a pie into quarters and gave 75% of it to your best friend, you would have half left.

F. You would have one quarter (25%) left.

4. 2100 hours is the same as 9 pm.

T. 2100 hours is the 24-hour-clock version of 9 pm.

5. Three is an odd number.

T

6. 3 is also a prime number.

T

7. Maths is everywhere.

T. The world around us is full of never-ending patterns and maths helps us see these patterns.

8. 2 is a prime number.

T

9. If you think of any two numbers, you can always find a number in between them.

T. There are infinite numbers between any two numbers because we can always make smaller and smaller divisions. For example, between 1 and 2 are 1.1, 1.01, 1.001 and more!

Add up all the numerals on this page. Don't forget to include the page number.

The answer is: 2449 (1 + 2 + 10 + 4 + 39 + 62 + 16 + 3 + 75 + 4 + 2100 + 9 + 5 + 3 + 6 + 3 + 7 + 8 + 2 + 9 + 81)

Page 83:

I eat 60 ice creams in one year

I will have eaten 4800 ice creams by the time I am eighty.

Page 97:

Page 104-105:

Sirocco
A hot, dry wind that blows from the Sahara Desert into Africa and Italy.

Aeolian
These winds shape the surface of the earth and create things like sand dunes.

Gale
This is a strong, fast-moving wind. Hold on to your hat!

Zephyr
A gentle breeze.

Squall
A stormy wind that can bring rain or snow.

Wuther
This wind howls across the moors.

Haboob
This can whip up a sandstorm.

Mistral
A cold wind that blows over the Mediterranean coast.

Brickfielder
A hot and dry Australian wind.

Southerly Buster
This sudden, cool wind comes, unsurprisingly, from the south.

Williwaw
Brrr. This is a stormy cold wind that blasts down mountainsides.

Willy-willy
A whirly, twirly Australian wind that whisks up dust devils.

```
C  M  N  B  V  C  X  Z  L  C  T  A  S  D  F  G
L  J  K  L  O  I  U  Y  T  L  H  R  E  W  C  Q
O  A  S  D  F  Z  B  F  Q  O  U  Z  D  F  L  H
U  D  B  E  C  L  O  U  D  U  N  G  L  W  O  P
D  Q  W  T  A  J  K  Z  C  D  D  A  T  P  U  A
I  G  S  Q  G  H  Z  D  F  S  E  X  S  C  D  V
N  M  B  V  C  X  Z  A  S  C  R  Q  D  W  L  A
E  A  S  D  F  G  H  J  K  A  C  L  U  M  E  N
S  E  W  Q  D  A  Y  Z  X  P  L  C  O  V  S  B
S  R  T  Y  U  D  I  O  P  E  O  L  L  K  S  Z
B  G  H  M  U  K  L  I  U  S  U  T  C  R  E  Q
V  J  D  O  A  L  S  G  T  F  D  H  E  L  Q  T
W  E  L  Y  P  Y  A  O  V  G  Q  U  S  R  E  W
Q  C  I  C  L  O  U  D  B  E  R  R  I  E  S  H
Z  A  H  U  Q  S  H  R  K  I  S  M  N  D  F  I
H  C  O  C  L  O  U  D  L  E  T  I  U  Y  T  R
```

Page 113:

1. thunder

2. cloud

3. loud

4. throne

5. odd

6. noddle

7. lunch

8. hunt

9. lord

10. curl

Page 117:

1. 1400 litres

2. 52 weeks

3. 72,800 litres

4. Answers will vary. Multiply your age by 72,800 litres.

5. Answers will vary. Multiply the number of people in your family by 1400.

Page 129:

48 squares

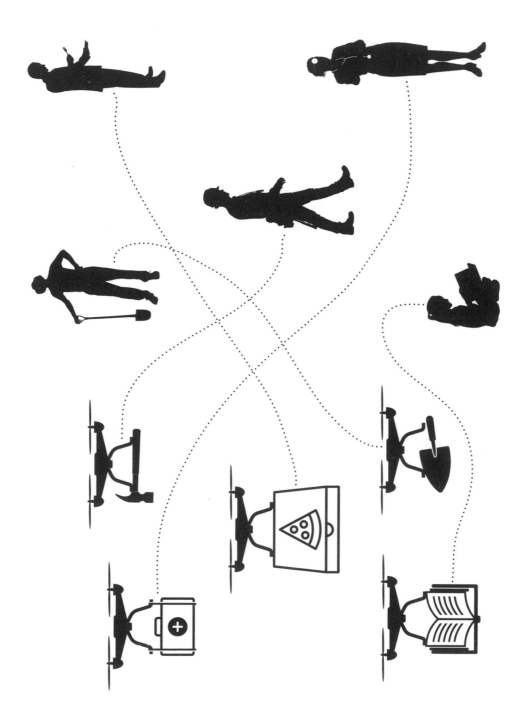

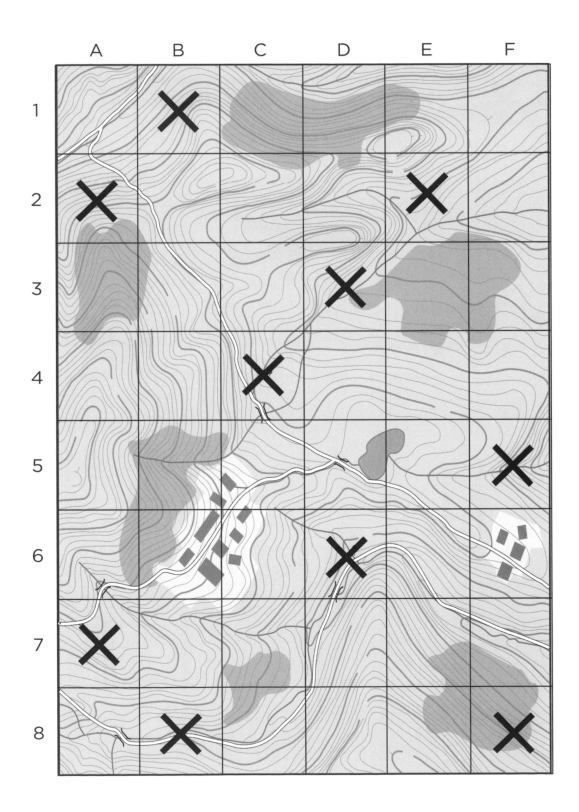

Page 140:

You can make the journey in 25 squares. Here is one version of that path.

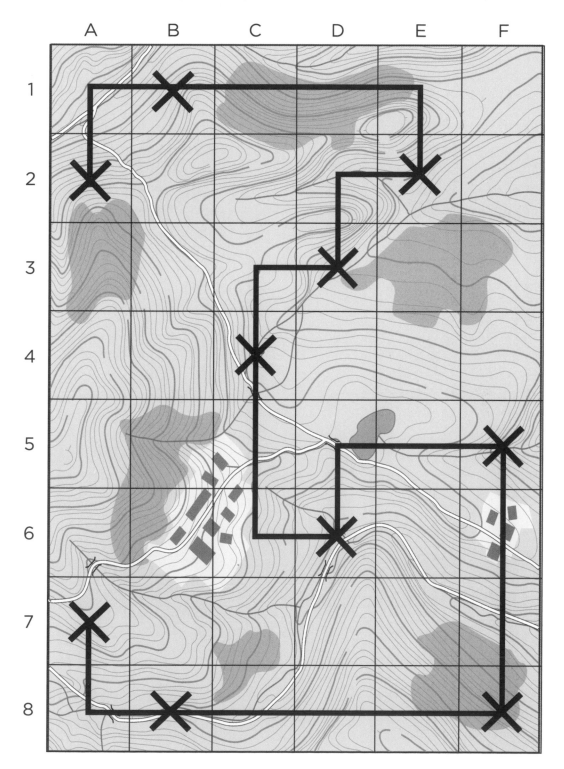

pear

pineapple

banana

blueberries

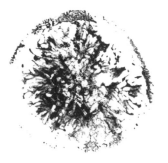

orange

apple

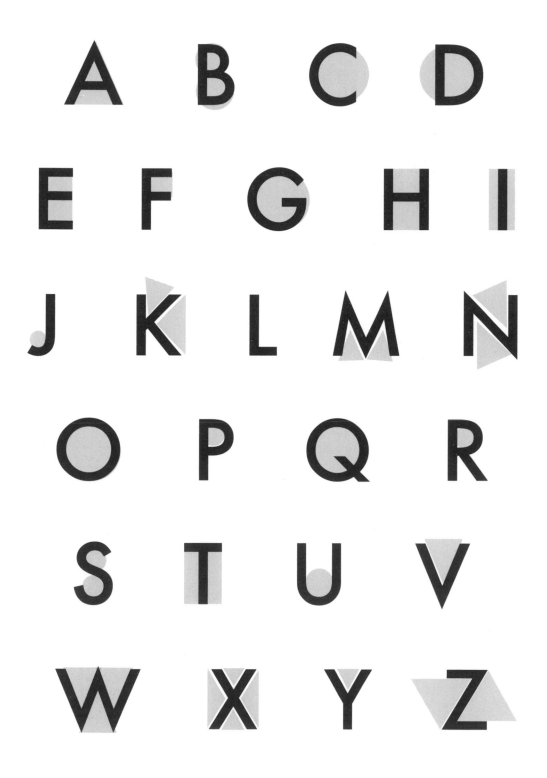

More fun for you

Even more fun for you